Lightbulb Thoughts

Noni Davidson

BookLeaf Publishing

India | USA | UK

Lightbulb Thoughts © 2023 Noni Davidson

All rights reserved.

No part of this publication may be reproduced, stored in a retrieval system, or transmitted, in any form or by any means, electronic, mechanical, photocopying, recording or otherwise, without the prior written permission of the presenters.

Noni Davidson asserts the moral right to be identified as the author of this work.

Presentation by *BookLeaf Publishing*

Web: www.bookleafpub.com

E-mail: info@bookleafpub.com

ISBN: 9789358369182

First edition 2023

DEDICATION

To the people in my life who've always supported me, including but not limited to my sister, my best friend and my discord community. Thank you for helping me learn to love myself and sticking around for it.

ACKNOWLEDGEMENT

To my past self for getting here. Here's another dream for us. We made it.

Falling

It'd be a lie to say that I ever had any intent of
falling for you and yet
And yet
Somehow I fell

I got blindsided by your smile and your laugh
The way I'd catch you looking when you think I
couldn't see

I fell in love with you almost shamelessly
The world could have ended and I would've just
been lost in you

Late-night calls and stolen moments
Nothing ever felt like enough

Falling was almost my favorite part of loving
you because it was fast
It was easy
Gave me butterflies and stupid smiles
Made me forget

Shameless beautiful consuming love
All because I fell

Outkast

On the outskirts of love
Of everything good and pure and right
OutKasted by the simple fact I was different

Preferred lurking in the shadows
Being unseen

Used to being called when people needed
something and not much else
Used to not believing people when they called
me pretty
Used for my body
Used for my skills

Started to think maybe that would be all I'm
good for
Because society deemed it so

Yet I was still somehow never quite enough
Just a little too much
Too loud
Too outspoken

Til I got pushed to the outskirts even more and
got quiet in the attempts to fit in to my
surroundings

Or even not enough
Not pretty enough
Not smart enough

I craved everyone else's validation to the point
where being an outkast is all I know now

And it's hard to come back from that

Obsession

I'm not sure I know how to love

Not at least, in the way most people know love.

I know the love you read in romance books, but
not the super cheesy holiday ones with the white
picket fence some kids and a dog

I only know obsessive all-consuming smothering
love.
And gods was I obsessed

The type that would bring a man to his knees,
burn the world for you kind of love

The type to where the level of possessive is
wearing your lover's marks prominently and
proudly

The kind that I would hand you a match if you
wanted the world to burn obsessed

The type of love the world feels is unhealthy
with how consumed you'd be in each other

I don't know how to love without obsession the
two are so intertwined I get bored when it's not

I stopped regretting it and started accepting it

Accepted that I had the power to make a man
borderline obsessed and bring him to his knees.

Accepted that my life is a series of revolving
doors and they always come back

Accepted that it's the type of love that scares
people

Accepted that, at least for a time it's not the most
inviting love

So I keep to myself always toeing the line in
hopes that maybe someday someone like that
will love me back

Funnel the obsession in healthy ways because I
seem to be in a world that wants me to fail

And I refuse to fail

Stay

Stay
Please stay

Just one more minute
One more hour
One more day

Stay here with me
Don't leave me
I don't want to be alone

I can't lose you
I can't have another heartbreak

Stay because I'm selfish
Stay because I love you

I need you

I don't want to start another cycle
I don't want to start over
I don't want to put mental flowers on another
grave
I don't want to have more ghosts to remember

Forgot the way a laugh sounds

I'm sorry

I know you are hurting
I know nobody understands

I'd rather be here for a thousand phone calls
Hear you cry and rant a million times

Stay
Just a little longer
Please stay

First love

When I think back to who I was before you
The girl who was always laughing and wasn't
afraid of the world
The girl I was before I had got my heart broken
Before I met you
It scares me
She was so full of light and hope
Didn't have such a pessimistic view of what the
world had turned out to be
I wish I could protect her
Protect the light inside so that no one had a
chance to dim it
But
It didn't feel real
She doesn't feel real
She fell in love with her firsts because she didn't
know what it was like to be hurt by the world yet
Nothing made more sense than falling for you
Because it felt different
It felt right
It felt worth the leap of faith it would take
But I was scared
I didn't want you to look back after and have
regrets
I didn't want you to look back and be hurt by me

To feel foolish for ever falling in love with me
I wanted your first love to be as great as it was
in the movies and the books you saw
As special and as permanent
But I didn't know how to love like that because I
had never been loved like that
Nor would I even know how to receive it if I
was to get it now.
Wanting it just
Wasn't enough

Fragments

I cling to the fragments, the small pieces that
make up my existence
Spent so long looking for myself in other people
I don't know who I am outside that anymore

Gone is the girl who only existed within the
limitations of the world
The one who spent so much time only smiling
for other people that her spark started to dim

I'm trying to figure out who I became so I can
figure out who I actually am

Spread my wings in an attempt to fly after being
limited for so long
Starting to not listen to people saying I'm not
capable because if I want it there's another way

Started to heal
So I don't have to be fragments held together by
spite and dreams unspoken

With a little glue and a lot of sleepless nights

Trying to heal the inner child that had to grow
up too fast
That teenager who thought she'd never make it

Baby steps to a brighter future

Regrets

He was never really mine you know

Someone who existed on the outskirts of my
being
Just barely out of reach

Timing was never right for us both pulled in the
directions of life our connection was temporary

But gods was it a whirlwind while it was here

Got lost in the intoxicating escape of would have
and could have beens no matter how unrealistic
we were drunk on the feeling

He was never really mine but still somehow it
hurt when he left
Now instead of the feeling of hope it was one of
regret

Because I should've known better
Wanted better for myself

But it was easy
It was familiar

And then it was gone
Almost as if it had never existed in the first
place

I don't regret falling I regret staying
Hoping it would change when I knew it
wouldn't
Feeling heartbroken when I knew I wasn't going
to be first

Going back in circles just wishing
I could go back and do it all again

But life goes on you know?
All you can do is go with it

Learning

Learning to live with it
The odds being stacked against you
Live in a system that sometimes feels designed
for you to fail
Learning that sometimes there is going to be
nothing you can do
That you can't help everyone
Can't save everyone
And choosing to pick optimism anyway
Choosing strength anyway
Choosing life anyway
Is more difficult than anyone will ever give
credit for

Journeys

Sometimes it's not even about the destination but
the journey
The way you got from point a to b and the stories
that accompany it
The way you persevered and fought for what you
wanted
The lessons you'll walk out the other side with
The advice you'll be able to give

About the people you'll meet
You'll love
Maybe lose

The memories you'll make

And when you finally make it there the journey is
what you'll look back on

When you thought you'd never make it
When you thought you should give up
When you thought there was no way you were
strong enough

All the times you got knocked down
People didn't believe in you
You did it
And what a hell of a ride it was

Goodbyes

So many goodbyes I never got to say
So many things I wish I could say to the people
no longer in my life

I love you
I'm sorry
I hope you are doing ok
I miss you
I didn't mean to hurt you

Goodbye
See you later
See you in another life

I hope you are happy
I hope you heal
I hope you get what you want in life

Goodbye
Good luck

To the ones I loved
And the ones I didn't

The ones who left on good terms
And on bad

Goodbye

Memories

The memories are dangerous all consuming
Overwhelming
Suffocating

Have the ability to pull you back from all the
progress you made
Everything you thought you healed from
Everything you thought you escaped

Your mind will block you sometimes to protect
you
Protect you from stuff you could handle
Stuff that should've broken you given the
chance

Memories that used to taste so sweet on your
tongue go sour
Memories that used to hurt so bad to think about
all of a sudden you are ok

Perspective shifts and the voices change

Stuff you thought was buried all of a sudden
comes to light

Stuff you thought you healed from only changed
form in how it hurts you

The older you get the harder it is to hold on to
happy and positive
But how else are you supposed to make it
through

Out of order

"Oh look at her" they say

"So attention seeking" they say

"She'll never get in or amount to anything"

Funny
So out of place she feels that she doesn't even try
anymore
She doesn't go out of her way to communicate or
interact

And yet somehow they say more about her than
when she was

They say she's different because they don't
understand why she dyed her hair
Why she wears bright colored makeup but the rest
of her wardrobe is mostly void of it
Why she wears baggy clothes

So out of place she feels she walks around with
headphones in head down ignoring the world
Just trying to make it through

Out of place means you make places for yourself
Safe spaces where physical or mental
Just to make it through

Poison

Didn't know loving you would poison me

Wrap me so deeply in loving you
That I had no chance of escape

That even after I'd think about you
That my memories will be so full of you

All of a sudden all the songs became about you
All of a sudden silly memories came rushing back
All of a sudden I blinked and I was alone

I had to learn to live without you

Try not to reopen wounds every time I saw
something that reminded me of you

Rewrite the way I felt so that I wouldn't hurt
anymore

Gods I loved you and would've done anything for
you

Now I don't even know how to love anyone but
myself like that anymore

Healing

I didn't want to have to heal from them
I didn't want to rearrange my life without them in
it
I didn't want to lose trust in myself and my ability
to pick people to be in my life

No one wants that
No one wants to lose someone who they thought
would be in their life forever

Healing sucks
Healing from something you never thought you'd
have to heal from is worse

People come and go
You live and you learn

You learn to pick up the pieces they left and glue
them back together
You learn how to be there for yourself
To have your own back when no one else will have
it for you

And you heal
You make the best of the hand you've been dealt
And you just
Figure it out

Apologies

I'll be honest
I don't want your apologies
They just taste like bitter sour meaningless
words to me

I don't have the capacity to believe that after
putting me through all you did that you're
actually sorry

There is no possible way after I begged you for
ages to feel remorse or anything about what
happened that now you are sorry

After I moved on
After I spent all that time healing from you

I tried being the bigger person but all that
brought me was more heartache and tears

So I walked away
I walked away because I was tired of being hurt
and knew I deserved better

So I'm sorry but you don't get to be sorry

You don't get to waltz in with your pretty done
up words and pretend you aren't doing this for
you
You don't get to make it all better because you
suddenly decided you need to clear your
conscious

I don't want your apologies so save them for
someone else

Because of you really changed there's probably
someone who needs it just as bad

Secrets

I feel like I have so many secrets

And it's not exactly even on purpose I just
Don't openly share a whole lot with most people

So some stuff will come as a surprise when it's
found out because not everyone knows

Air of mystery is something everyone agrees on
Or the ask of why else would she stick to herself if
not to hide something

I'm not even exactly trying to hide things I'm just
private
Don't feel the need to have all my business out in
the street all the time

I hold more secrets of other people
Some of which don't even really matter anymore
But people always say they find me easy to talk to

So a girl of mystery and full of secrets is what I've
become
And a girl full of mystery and secrets I'll probably
remain

Living

I'm in some weird limbo of living to survive and
actually living

Trying to heal and work through trauma pockets
while living in the middle of them

Trying to find some semblance of a life when
there's no one left in it

Trying to not simply just throw myself into work
or into breaking down

Trying to remember what actually feelings are

Trying to walk out into the world everyday and
present some version of a person

But it's not really living is it?

Just waking up to go through the motions

Waking up trying to pretend to feel like a person

I'm tired of surviving but I can't find where the
transition to living is supposed to be

Honestly

Honestly it kinda sucks

Time

All I needed was time
Just a little more time to love
Just a little more time to exist in that bubble
before being thrown out into the world

I barely remember it
The time before that bubble popped and reality
came crashing in
The time before self-awareness and weird
pockets of memories that match voices that
aren't mine

Wanted time to learn and do all the things before
I graduated
Wanted time with my siblings before they didn't
want to hang out with me anymore

We have an abundance of time that moves fast
and doesn't stop
And we're just going along with the ride and yet
we do everything in our power to slow it down
Even though we know we can't

Perception

Perception is the way you see the world
Because we're human often our perception is
skewed

Whether because we don't want to look at
what's staring us straight in the face
Or we choose not to

Self-awareness can also screw with perception
I'm either hyper-aware or oblivious to what's
happening depending on the day

I'll gaslight myself into believing that things are
ok
Only then to be wrong

Perception is a funny ever-changing set of things
Changes understanding and viewpoint at the
drop of a hat sometimes

Can't decide if I'm better or worse for it

Breathe

Breathe
Just breathe

Deep breath four in four out

Name five things you can see
Can touch
Can hear
Can smell

Breathe deep enough you come back to reality
And get out of your head

I know it's rough
The world feels almost suffocating at times
But I believe in you

Hope

Hope for the future
Hope in that things will change no matter how
bad
Hope that you can keep seeing the light at the
end of the tunnel

Hope keeps us going
Hope in change
In a better life

Hope in change
In healing
In finding people who love you for you

Slowly getting hope back
Slowly starting to build that back up around the
people who love me

And I'm happier for it

www.ingramcontent.com/pod-product-compliance
Lightning Source LLC
LaVergne TN
LVHW010951200726

843509LV00013B/2364